MW00604598

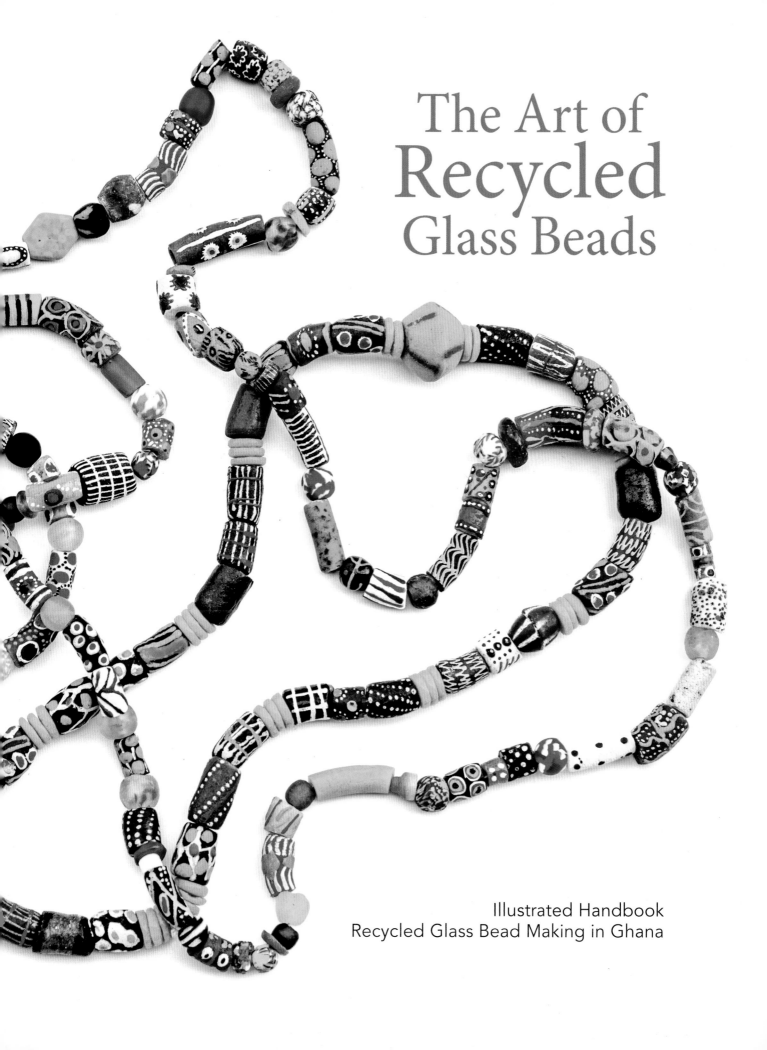

The Art of
Recycled
Glass Beads

Illustrated Handbook
Recycled Glass Bead Making in Ghana

The Art of Recycled Glass Beads

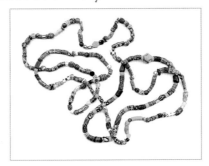

Illustrated Handbook
Recycled Glass Bead Making in Ghana

© 2020
Philippe J. Kradolfer/Nomoda E. Djaba

All rights reserved

Ghana-Art Publications Ltd/EPP Books Services

Design and Photography by
Philippe J. Kradolfer/Regula B. Kradolfer
www.pjkradolfer.com

Master Bead Maker Nomoda E. Djaba
cedibeadsindustry@yahoo.com

Special assistance by:
Obedient O. Ankrah/Bryan Crockett/Sofia Spannaus

Any use of this material beyond those allowed by the exemption in
U.S. copyright law, such as section 107 "Fair Use" and section 108
"Library Copying," require the written permission of the authors.

ISBN 978-1-7923-2241-9

Printed in Malaysia

Contents

Translucent glass beads

Bodom beads

Powder glass glazed beads

Chevron beads

Bi-cone powder glass glazed beads

Flame-worked bead

Note: Images of beads throughout this book are enlarged to show detail and are not necessarily actual size and were manufactured by different bead makers.

Introduction

Ghana is one of the largest producers of beads in Africa, with the Krobo people being one of the main producers and innovators of recycled glass bead manufacturing. With its wealth of history, evolution, and growth, Ghana's bead making tradition dates back centuries.

Besides being used as personal ornaments, recycled glass beads in Ghana have an important cultural, religious, and social significance.

Originally, beads were mainly worn by traditional kings or chiefs and queen mothers to display their social status and wealth during ceremonies, rites, rituals, and local festivals. Their use today has extended well beyond their ancestral usage becoming part of the Ghanaian identity, and reaching a worldwide audience.

People all over the world have found a way to express their individuality through these small, unique, and powerful pieces of art.

The process of recycled glass beads begins with used bottles or scrap glass which go through a labor intensive manual process of selection, cleaning, breaking or pulverizing, firing, cooling, and polishing.

Although this publication covers many important and essential aspects of the recycled glass bead techniques, it is only a small window into the vast world of bead making. It will take the reader on a journey of discovery and will invoke amazement at the ingenuity and dedication of bead makers of the past and present.

Nomoda Ebenezer Djaba, better known as *Cedi*, is an internationally recognized figure in the world of recycled glass bead making and one of Ghana's most prominent bead makers. In this book, he shares technical skills of this ancient, and at the same time, modern art with an invitation to discover this craftsmanship.

Cedi at his workshop in Odumase Krobo in the Eastern Region of Ghana.

Antique Venetian trade beads like the *Mosaic* also called *Millefiori*, the wound glass with polychrome or compound trailed decorations, the striped four layers star bead, among others, have greatly contributed to the art of recycled glass beads in Ghana.

CHAPTER 1
A Short History of Ghanaian Beads

The word *bead* is derived from the Old English word of Germanic origin *gebed*, and the Latin word *bene*, meaning prayer.

Beads are some of the oldest handmade objects used throughout centuries by many cultures as religious objects, such as for prayer, as currency or trade, and as personal adornment.

The Ghanaian glass bead making tradition is one of several regional glass bead making traditions in West Africa, and all of these traditions evolved over many centuries in the context of long distance trade. Transcontinental trade over the Sahara from the 8th century and ocean-going trade from the 1480s transferred finished beads as well as raw materials for glass bead production. They also introduced knowledge of various methods of working beads and glass.

Interregional trade provided networks for sharing local and transcontinental bead making technologies. Bead artists in the coastal and southern regions of modern Ghana created their own distinctive mold-form powder glass bead making processes from widely shared knowledge of drawn powder glass bead technologies of West Africa's interregional and trans-Saharan trade centers.[1]

Bead making in Ghana was first documented by John Barbot in 1746.[2] However, the importance of beads was well established in West Africa long before the arrival of the Europeans on the coast at the end of the 15th century.[3]

The great majority of powder glass beads produced today are made by Ashanti and Krobo craftsmen and women. Krobo bead making has been documented to date from as early as the 1920s, but despite limited archaeological evidence, it is believed that Ghanaian powder glass bead making dates further back. With a rich history of evolution and growth spanning several centuries, Ghanaian recycled glass bead making and trade are an important part of Ghanaian culture and economy and are well recognized worldwide.

Since the sixteenth century, glass bead making in sub-Saharan Africa has been concentrated in today's Niger, Nigeria, and Ghana. This tradition remains intact, and today the Bida of Nigeria and Krobo of Ghana are two of the most important African glass bead manufacturers.[4]

Beads have frequently been considered to be a symbolic representation of sacred knowledge, believed to possess curative powers, used as the fee for passage to the afterlife, and as prompters to ensure the proper conduct of rituals and prayers.

The aesthetic quality and value of Ghanaian beads are constantly improving through the initiative and creativity of the bead makers; however, the scale of bead making is still small and takes place almost entirely in thousands of small artisan workshops.

Although recycled glass beads in Ghana are made also by the Ashantis and Ewes, the Krobo beads are among the best made and most innovative, with many examples of intricate and artistic designs.

1 Gott, Suzanne, *Ghana's Glass Beadmaking Arts in Transcultural Dialogues*, 2014.
2 Barbot, J (1746), *A Voyage to New Calabar. Collection of Voyages and Travels*, Linot and Osborn (6 vols.): 455–467.
3 DeCorse, Christopher R. (1989), *Beads as Chronological Indicators in West African Archeology. Beads: Journal of the Society of Bead Researchers* (1:41-53).
4 Dubin, Lois Sherr, *The History of Beads*, p. 48.

Antique Trade Beads Gallery

Peoples on the West African coast began to trade with Europe in the late 15th century. First were the Portuguese, followed over the next four hundred years by the Dutch, English, French, Belgians, and Germans. They brought millions of Venetian, Dutch, and Bohemian glass beads to Africa.[1]

Antique polychrome *Eye* beads, also known as *Skunk* beads.

Antique layered small *Chevron* or *Star* beads.

Several types of antique wound compound glass with polychrome decorations.

Antique Venetian *Mosaic* or *Millefiori* beads.

---

1 Dubin, Lois Sherr, (1995) *The History of Beads*, p. 50.

The *Dipo* ceremony is a great occasion to exhibit rich, authentic, and beautifully handmade Krobo recycled glass beads.

CHAPTER 2
Beads in the Traditional Culture

Beads in Ghana have an important cultural, religious, and social significance. They have been attributed to bear symbolic representation of sacred knowledge. They are used in infant naming, puberty rites, weddings, traditional festivals, funerals, and as prompters in rituals and prayers. They are worn as a status symbol, used as amulets, and have been traded for precious commodities. Sometimes they are believed to possess curative powers.

Among the ceremonies or rituals in which beads play a significant role we find the *Puberty rite* known as *Dipo.* During this traditional ceremony, especially among the Krobos, in the Eastern Region of Ghana, participating girls are adorned with large amounts of captivating beads.

These beads have often been passed down through many generations and are a symbol of a family's wealth and status. The family's heirloom is often complemented with the purchase of additional beads for the graduating initiate.

The *Dipo* ceremony—one of the most important events of the year—held annually, symbolizes a girl's coming of age into womanhood.

In recent years, this ceremony has changed from an initiation process and schooling that lasted an entire year, to rites and ceremonies lasting 4 days, including community gatherings and celebrations.

On the last day of *Dipo*, the girls assemble at the village common, wearing their best clothes as well as multiple strands of beads around the neck with a heavy girdle around the waist, made of several layers of beads with a weight of up to 25 kilos (55 lbs).

The color of the beads is important for the occasion. Yellow beads are often used to represent wealth, maturity, prosperity, and long life. Blue beads are associated with affection and tenderness. A combination of white and blue beads evokes femininity.

On the last day of *Dipo*, the girls gather at the village common, wearing their best clothes as well as multiple strands of beads around the neck, arms, and waist.

Dipo girls during a procession, wearing multiple strands of beads around their waist with a weight of up to 25 kilos (55 lbs).

Sometimes younger girls in the family (ages 6 to 18) also go through the ceremony along with their older sisters, as it is less costly if the younger ones go through with their elder sisters.[1]

1 Huber, Hugo, *The Krobo, Traditional, Social and Religious Life of a West African People*, 1963

Beautifully adorned girl with beads during the *Asogli Te Za* or *Yam* Festival in Ho, Volta Region.

Children wearing bead necklaces and bracelets are an essential part of many ceremonies and festivals. They also are adorned with beads in school functions and church services. These children are participating in the *Hogbetsotso* Festival of the *Anlo* people in the Volta Region.

The use of beads in traditional festivals such as the *Amufest* of the Avatime Traditional Area, the *Ngmayem* Festival of the Manya Krobo Traditional Area, the *Te Za* or *Yam* Festival of the Asogli State, the *Ewe Kente* Festival of the Agotime Traditional Area, the *Hogbetsotso* Festival in the Anloga Traditional Area, and many others, is a sign of their importance and wide use across Ghana.

Nene Sakite II is the Paramount Chief of the Manya Krobo Traditional Area, in the Eastern Region of Ghana, where *Cedi Beads* factory is located. Nene Sakite II is wearing *Akorso Bodom* beads in his bracelet and necklace.

Originally beads were mainly worn by traditional kings or chiefs and queen mothers to display their social status and wealth during ceremonies, rites, rituals, and local festivals. Their use today has grown beyond their ancestral usage and have become part of the Ghanaian identity. Paramount chiefs, chiefs and queen mothers still today proudly wear their best regalia which often includes beautiful recycled glass bead necklaces and bracelets. Traditional priests and priestesses also wear recycled glass beads in form of necklaces and bracelets as part of their priestly attire.

The color of the bottles and cathedral or stained scrap glass has a direct relationship to the color of the final bead. To obtain secondary colors, ceramic pigment needs to be added to the primary color of the pulverized glass.

CHAPTER 3
Recycled Glass

The process of recycled glass beads begins with used glass bottles or scrap glass which go through a labor intensive manual process of selection, washing and cleaning, breaking or pulverizing, firing, shaping, grinding, polishing, and stringing.

The type of beads to be produced determines the glass to be used, either crushed or pulverized glass, old broken beads, or imported seed beads. Crushed glass, also known as *frit,* is generally between 1 to 5 mm in size. Powder glass is made using a metal mortar with a pestle to pulverize the glass. The pulverized glass is then sifted to obtain a very fine powder with a size of 0.13 to 0.25 mm. The powder glass is mixed with ceramic pigment to create desired additional colors.

Different types of glass expand or contract at different rates. This is known as the Coefficient of Thermal Expansion (COE). The range of the COE for powder glass or *frit* varies between 96 and 104. Due to this difference it is important to verify the compatibility of each type of glass. Even bottles of the same color but different brands may have a different COE.

Old or used bottles ready to be transformed into beads.

As bead manufacturing uses different kinds of glass, it is important to experiment with temperature and time to obtain optimal results. To test the compatibility, a few beads of a given type of glass or a combination of them may be fired. The glass should always be of similar COE in the same mold. After annealing, if the glass is compatible with one another, the beads will turn out well without cracking or breaking.

Car windshield or tempered glass can never be used for bead manufacturing.

Recycled powder glass beads take 20 to 35 minutes at a temperature of 600° to 800° C (1112° to 1472° F). For translucent beads made with *frit,* it takes 30 to 45 minutes at 800° to 1000° C (1472° to 1832° F).

The use of a pyrometer is recommended to reach and maintain the right temperature of the kiln; nevertheless, most bead makers in Ghana rely only on their experience.

The wood used for firing plays an important role for the kiln to reach the right glass transition temperature. The best results are obtained using hard and dried wood.

It is important to know the time it takes for glass to cool down as the glass may crack in the cooling process. Depending on the size of the bead and weather conditions, the cooling down period will be between 1 and 1.5 hours. It is important to let the beads cool down naturally in the molds.

As making recycled glass beads is a manual process, the bead maker needs to find the right balance between the number of beads in each mold, the number of molds in the kiln, the size of the kiln, and the timing and temperature to manufacture the "perfect" bead.

In addition to the balance between these factors, patience and practice are of great value as there are steps in the process that must not be rushed. They need to follow the natural process of firing and cooling. Over time, careful and methodical bead makers can develop the skills needed to become *master bead makers.*

Crushed Glass Process

1. Used bottles are cleaned and washed.

2. Bottles are carefully broken into smaller pieces.

3. Crushed glass is obtained with a small hammer.

4. Crushed glass ready to be poured in the mold.

5. Crushed glass placed in the mold.

6. Molds with crushed glass ready for the kiln.

7. Mold with crushed glass being placed in the kiln.

8. Molds being fired.

9. Beads shaped using metal pins.

10. Beads being washed after the grinding process.

11. Upon cleaning and polishing, the transformation to bead has been completed.

12. Combination of different types and color of beads ready for stringing.

Powder Glass Process

1. Washed scrap glass ready to be pounded.

2. Glass pounded with a metal mortar and pestle.

3. Pounded glass sifted with a fine mesh.

4. Pigment mixed with powder glass.

5. Powder glass poured into the mold with a funnel.

6. Molds filled with powder glass ready to be fired.

7. Mold carefully placed in the kiln.

8. Mold with hot glass being shaped.

9. Beads being grinded.

10. Bead being polished with lubricant oil.

11. Upon cleaning and polishing, the transformation from powder glass to bead has been completed.

12. Combination of different types and color of beads ready for stringing.

Imported Seed Beads Process

 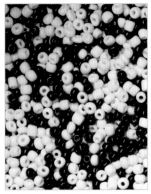  

1. Seed bead combinations.

2a. Seed beads placed in a 1–hole mold.

2b. Seed beads placed in a 8–hole mold.

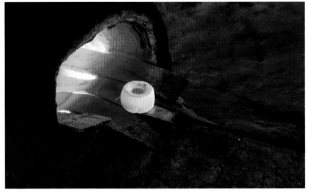

3. Mold with seed beads taken out of the kiln.

4. Hot bead being shaped into its final form.

5. Beads in their mold cooling down naturally.

6. Beads ready to be cleaned and polished.

7. Beads with soft sand ready for the grinding process.

8. Washed beads ready to be coated with lubricant oil.

9. Upon cleaning and polishing, the transformation from seed beads to a new bead has been completed.

10. Combination of different types and color of beads ready for stringing.

CHAPTER 4
Equipment, Tools, and Supplies

Most bead artisans in Ghana learn to make their own required tools and equipment needed to make traditional recycled glass beads.

The tools, equipment, and supplies shown here are the most typical used in the glass bead recycling industry across Ghana.

Bead making is still done mainly at an artisan level in hundreds, if not thousands of small shops, with relatively simple equipment and tools following traditional methods.

Depending on local availability and circumstances, the equipment, tools, and supplies would need to be properly adapted.

Although most tools and equipment are handmade by the bead makers themselves, some of the tools and equipment can be purchased in local hardware stores.

Specialized equipment and tools required for Chevron and lamp-worked beads are mainly imported and are not shown in this chapter.

The glass used in the bead making industry comes from used bottles or scrap glass collected from diverse sources.

Tempered glass cannot be used in the recycled glass bead manufacturing process.

Kiln

The first step in creating a new bead workshop is the building of a kiln. The kiln is constructed from clay formed by termites for their colony structures.

Carved Bead Hole Template

Bead-hole templates are made of wood dowels. To have a consistent indent in the clay, a mark is made on the dowel.

Wooden Paddle/Bat

A wooden paddle/bat is used to shape and dress the clay mold.

Clay Mold

Molds give shape to the beads. A good design is essential for the consistent shape of the beads.

Kaolin

Kaolin is a soft, earthy, usually white clay mineral used to coat the mold to prevent the glass from sticking to the clay mold.

Glass

The process of recycled glass beads begins with used bottles or scrap glass which go through a labor intensive manual process.

Hammer

A hammer or small mallet is used to break the bottles and glass into small pieces known as *frit*.

Metal Mortar and Pestle

Glass is pulverized using a metal mortar with a sealed bottom and a metal pestle.

Sifter

A sifter with a very fine mesh is used to obtain the final powder glass.

Tin Funnel

Funnels are used to tip powder glass or *frit* into the molds. Different sized funnels help to keep glass colors separated and to control the amount poured.

Design or Wooden Pin

Wooden design sticks are used to transfer powder glass from the funnel to the mold and also to help shape the powder glass in the mold.

Dried Cassava Leaf Stalk

Dried or semi-dried cassava leaf stalk, straw grass, or any light wooden skewers are used in the molds as a place holder for the center hole of the bead.

Scissors or Cutting Blade

Scissors or cutting blades are used to cut the cassava leaf stalk, straw grass, or any light wooden skewer once placed as hole holders in the mold.

Thin Pin

A thin pin is used to make the thin holes for the vertical powder glass beads.

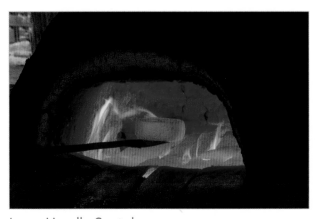

Long Handle Spatula

Long metal spatulas with a bamboo or wooden handle are used to transfer molds in and out of the kiln.

Metal Dowel/Awl/Spindle/Pin

Metal pins with a wooden handle are used to make the center hole of the bead, give shape to the bead and also to press the mold against the working surface.

Glazing Mixture

Beads are glazed or painted using a mixture of very fine powder glass, mixed with ceramic pigment and water.

Glazing or Painting Pin

Glazed beads are painted using a small drawing pin or the tip of a skewer dipped in a glazing mixture.

Polishing or Grinding Stone and Soft Sand

Soft sand is used on the polishing or grinding stone mixed with water to clean the beads from impurities and to polish them.

Electric Grinder

Alternatively, an electric grinder is used to touch up and polish some bead types.

Water

Clean water is used after the grinding process to wash the beads.

Lubricant Oil

Multi-purpose oil, baby oil, or Vaseline is used to remove the dry look of the beads after the grinding process and to give them a shiny appearance.

CHAPTER 5
Molds

Molds give shape to the beads; therefore, a good design is essential for the consistent shape of the beads and the life span of the mold. Although relatively simple to make, there are several elements, if not considered, that could affect the final quality of the bead.

Considerations to clay mold designs:

- Determine the size of the finished bead.
- The thickness of the sides and bottom of the mold should be about 1/3 of the thickness of the bead.
- Limit the number of holes to allow the shaping of all the beads before the glass cools down.
- Consider that powder glass and crushed glass when fired shrinks differently in the mold, thus the depth and width of the mold needs to be adjusted to obtain the finished desired size of the bead.
- For example, for a 25 mm (1 inch) round bead, the hole should be approximately 38 mm (1 1/2 inches) in width and depth with 13 mm (1/2 inch) to 25 mm (1 inch) of clay at the sides and bottom of the holes.

How to make clay molds:

- Molds are made using clay high in aggregates, like sand or grog, that contain a high percentage of silica and alumina that will fire to at least 1000° C (1832° F).
- Once the clay has been prepared, it should be periodically cut open to make sure the clay is homogenized and bubble free.
- The clay is then hand-shaped into a patty-like form.
- The clay is then kneaded with a circular motion to create an even texture, slapping it with a paddle on the working surface to remove any air that may have been trapped in the clay.
- While handling clay, it is kept moist by covering it with a damp cloth.
- The size of the patty depends on the size of the beads to be made.
- The patty for the mold should not be larger than 127 mm (5 inches) across, the average size being 76 to 102 mm (3 to 4 inches).
- The molds are sized so that they can be moved easily in and out of the kiln without tipping them over.

1. The clay is pounded with a wooden pestle in a wooden mortar to be made homogenized, malleable, and bubble free.

2. The pounded clay is formed into a large clay ball to start the process of forming the molds.

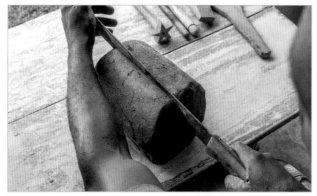

3. The clay ball is shaped into a cylindrical form and cut longitudinally in two or four pieces.

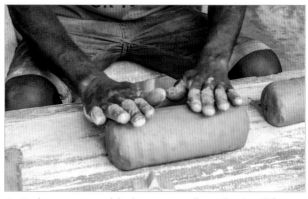

4. Each piece is molded into a smaller cylindrical form.

5. The cylinder is cut into shapes of 7 to 8 cm (2.7 to 3.1 inches) long by 6 to 7 cm (2.3 to 2.7 inches) wide.

6. The new cylinder formed is rounded using one hand and a small wooden paddle.

7. The circular shape is slapped with a wooden paddle to remove any air bubbles inside the mold.

8. A carved wood template is dipped in water to prevent it from sticking to the clay.

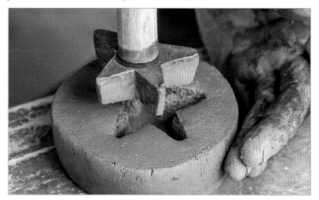

9. The template is carefully stamped into the clay to make the hole.

10. This mold is being made with 8 holes.

After the molds have been made, they are left at room temperature for about 24 hours. After this period, the exterior of the mold is re-touched or re-dressed. This includes re-patting with the wooden paddle and polishing the inside of the holes with a humidified, carved wooden bead template. After the redressing and before the molds are fired, they need to be completely dry. The molds are then left upside down in a dry place for one day.

On the second day, the mold is turned up again. This process allows air to circulate and dry the molds, preventing cracks.

On the third day, to speed up the process, the molds are placed in a ventilated area at room temperature for 1 to 3 days, depending on the weather conditions.

This is followed by 3 to 4 days of exposing the molds to sun light. The next day, the molds are placed upside down for 24 hours or more, if needed, depending on the weather conditions.

The following day the mold is reversed. After they have been well-dried in the sun, the molds go through the bisque process.

For the bisque process, the temperature of the kiln should be kept below the boiling point of water at 100° C (212° F). If above this point, the water in the clay will boil and may cause bubbles to break the mold.

Once the molds have been fired they need to be coated in kaolin to prevent the glass from sticking to the mold. Kaolin coating needs to be applied after each firing.

How to bisque fire clay molds:

- Place dried molds in the kiln.
- Heat the kiln to 71° C (160°F), letting molds dry in the kiln for 20 to 35 minutes.
- Increase temperature to 600° C (1112° F) for approximately 30 to 45 minutes.
- Increase temperature again to 1000° C (1832° F), holding at this temperature for 20 to 35 minutes.
- Put out the fire and let it cool down.
- Molds should not be removed until they can be comfortably touched by hand.

Molds in the drying phase before firing.

Coating sequence of the molds with kaolin.

How to coat the molds with kaolin:

- Pour 2 to 4 cups of water in a large container.
- Slowly sprinkle kaolin, mixing it with a stick, until a thin watery mixture is obtained.
- The mixture should cover the entire mold without soaking it.
- Take the mold out of the mixture and let it dry completely.
- Molds can be placed in a kiln at 100° to 150° C (212 ° to 302° F) to dry them faster. *(Optional)*.
- Once the coat of kaolin has dried, repeat the coating process 2 to 3 times for new molds to ensure the kaolin mixture covers the mold completely.
- Make sure the mixture is stirred before each use.
- Used molds should be coated only once.

Bead hole templates are made of a wooden dowel. To have a consistent indent in the clay in the shape of the bead template, it is important to make a depth mark. When making a bi-cone shape or a small waist bead, the template must have a small nub at the bottom. This nub forms a dimple in the clay which supports the cassava leaf stalk or straw grass bead-hole place holder. As an alternative, a bamboo skewer or any thin light wood can be used.

The molds on the table have been coated with kaolin and are ready to be used.

   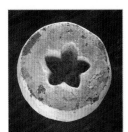 

Molds that have already been used look ivory, cream, or brownish, and they need to be re-coated in kaolin. Molds need to be re-coated with kaolin before every use to prevent the hot glass from sticking to the mold.

CHAPTER 6
Kilns

The kiln, traditionally known as *Mue Late* in the Krobo language, is constructed from clay formed by termites for their colony structures. These large rust-colored termite mounds are a dramatic feature of the southeastern Ghanaian landscape. The soil mixture made by the termites contains enzymes that act as a binding element, allowing the kiln to resist high temperatures.

The clay is brought to the site where the kiln will be built. Overnight, the clay will be softened with water. Using their feet the builders of the kiln will wedge or prepare the clay by softening it and eliminating air bubbles from it.

The lifespan of a kiln will vary depending on the type of beads fired. Melting powder glass will last 3 to 4 years, *frit* 2 to 3 years, and seed beads 3 to 5 years.

Termite mounds made of sand, clay, soil, and wood chips, fastened with termite saliva, rise up to 3 meters (9.8 ft) in height.

Elements of a Krobo kiln:

- The dome serves as the actual kiln with a front opening to introduce the molds and a back opening to introduce the wood for firing.
- The front is a solid clay platform that extends from beneath the front opening, serving as a pre-warming area to place bead molds and preventing anyone from getting too close to the fire.
- The floor is constructed from recycled car parts, which rest above a lower cavity where the wood burns.
- The flow of natural air has to be considered to control the heat and the reach of the flames. In some cases a front door is built to control the flow of air.
- It has an approximate height of 91 cm (3 ft) and a length of 76 cm (2 1/2 ft). The front platform extends another 76 cm (2 1/2 ft).

The front opening of the kiln allows the molds to be placed one by one to be fired.

Skilled kiln operators are able to place two molds at the same time.

Kiln temperatures reach up to 1000° C (1832° F).

The molds are placed in the kiln using a shovel-like tool or spatula made out of a long bamboo stick with a metal plate in the front.

Depending on the size of the molds and the kiln, 40 to 50 molds may be placed in a kiln at anyone time.

Neem, or Nimtree and Acacia are used as wood for kiln firing. As fast-growing trees, they are considered a weed in many places and are abundant in Ghana. However, any kind of hard dried wood could be used for firing the kiln.

The back of the kiln provides easy access to introduce the needed firewood to heat the kiln or to remove the wood, charcoal, or ashes to cool down the kiln.

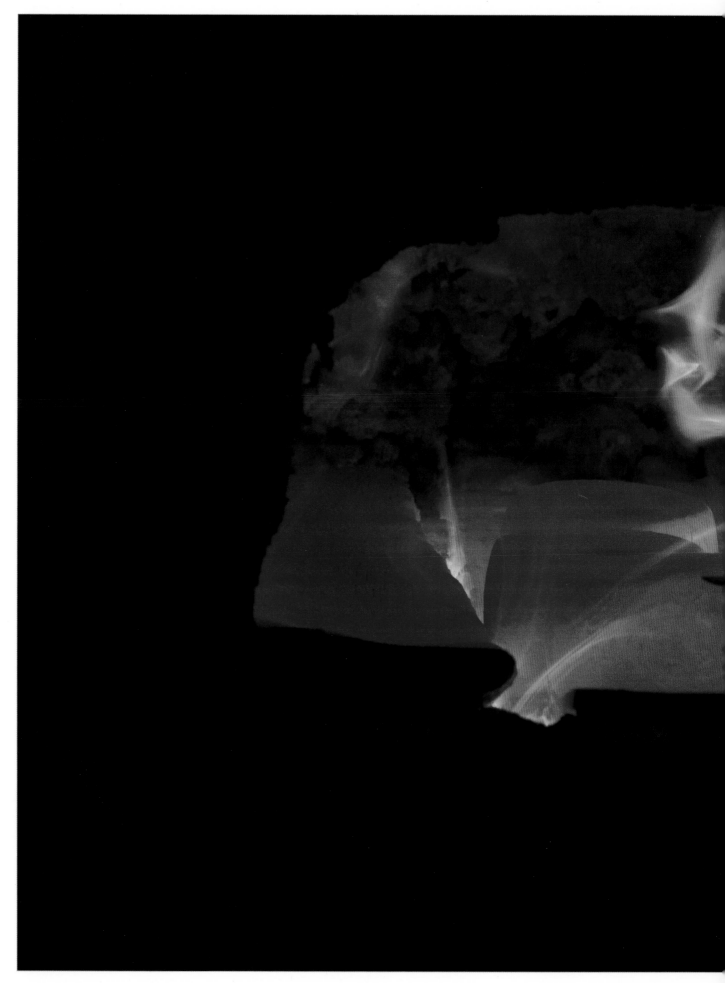

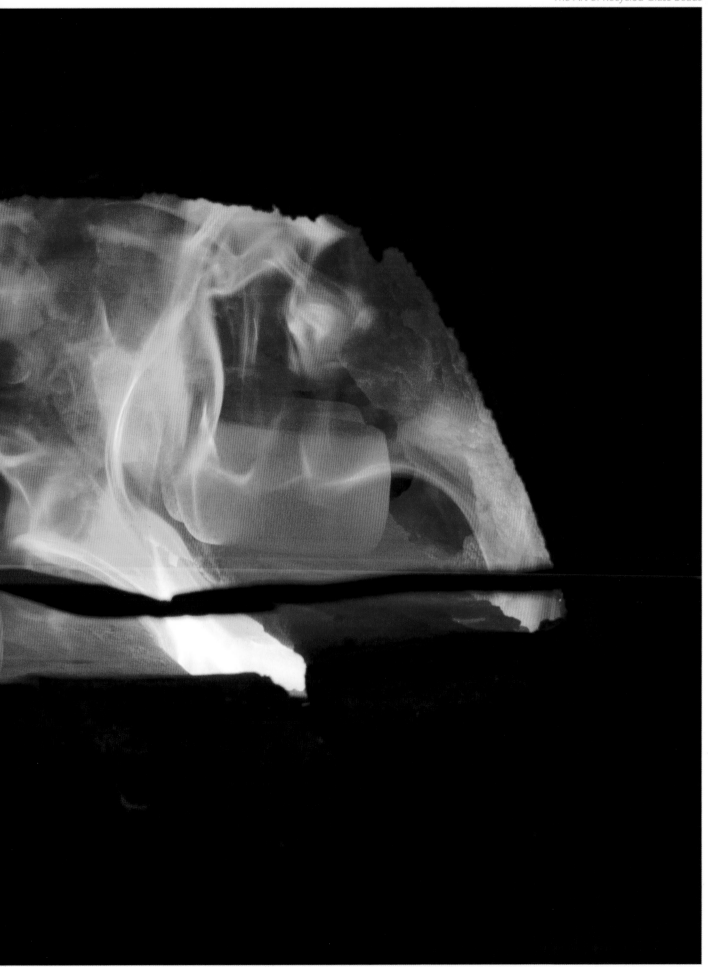

CHAPTER 7
Powder Glass Beads

Powder glass beads are made using pulverized glass. Powder glass is obtained by crushing used bottles or scrap glass with a metal mortar and a pestle. The pulverized glass is then sifted to obtain a fine powder glass. The powder glass is mixed with ceramic pigment to obtain different colors.

There are different types of powder glass beads depending on the design. Powder glass beads, inspired by European striped drawn glass beads, are produced using vertical-axis molds one by one. After filling the bead chambers with powder glass, a needle-like tool is used to make channels in the powder along the bead chamber walls, which are then filled with contrasting colored powder glass.

While handling powder glass, facial and hand protection should be worn at all times as glass powder can irritate eyes, nose, and mouth.

How to make powder glass beads:

- Place a small cassava leaf stalk or alternative in each hole of the desired mold.
- Tip or pour powder glass into the mold all the way to the top of the mold using the design pin and funnels.
- Tap the filled mold slightly.
- Depending on the design of the bead, other colors needed are slowly added with a thin pin and small funnels.
- Place the mold in the kiln for 10 to 15 minutes at a temperature of 200° to 300° C (392° to 572° F).
- Gradually increase the temperature up to 600° to 800° C (1112° to 1472° F) for 20 to 35 minutes depending on the dryness and quality of the firewood.
- Shape the beads using the technique shown in *Chapter 14*.
- Follow the same cleaning and polishing steps as shown in *Chapter 15*.

Cassava leaf stalk is placed in each hole as a place holder for the bead hole.

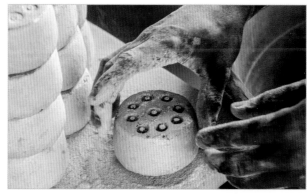

Mold set with cassava leaf stalk ready to be filled with powder glass.

Powder glass is poured in the mold using a funnel.

Molds ready to be fired in the kiln.

Powder Glass Bead Types

Bi-cone beads, also called King beads (*Olongo*), are divided into three major categories:

These beads are made of two single cone beads stacked together with a pressing motion at the base of each other, thus forming a single bead. The mold is placed back in the kiln to finish the fusing process. Once the mold is brought out of the kiln, the bead is pressed once more to ensure the complete fusion. The mold gives them the cone shape. The mold has an even number of holes as each bead is made of two half cone beads.

King bead

1. Eye Beads

For the mold-form powder glass versions of the lamp-work Venetian eye beads, the bead maker inserts pre-cast powder glass eyes on the walls of each bead chamber while filling the chamber with powder glass. Eye beads can also be made using the glaze or direct pouring method.

Pre-cast eyes   Glazed eyes

2. Spider Web Beads (*Anansi*)

These beads are made using the same process as the horizontal-stripe beads combined with the vertical bead process. Once the horizontal bead has been created, a very thin stick is inserted at the edge of the mold towards the bottom, pouring a contrasting powder glass color. Spider web beads can also be made using the glaze or direct pouring method.

Spider web bead known as *Anansi* bead.

3. King or Royal Beads

These beads are made using the same process as the horizontal-stripe beads combined with the vertical bead process. Once the horizontal bead has been created, a thin stick is inserted at the edge of the mold towards the bottom, pouring a contrasting powder glass color. These beads can also be made using the glaze or direct pouring method.

Direct King Bead   Glazed King Bead

Disk Beads (*Taka or Ntaka*)

The disk or *Taka* beads are made following the same technique as all powder glass beads. The main difference is that these beads are turned over in the mold while they are *semi-done* after 20 to 30 minutes at 500° to 750° C (932° to1382° F). They are then placed again in the kiln for another 25 to 30 minutes. Once out of the kiln they are pressed against the bottom of the mold with an inverted nail tool.

Disk, *Taka*, or *Ntaka* beads

Horizontal-Striped Beads (*Keta Awuazi*)

The stripes of these beads run perpendicular to the bead hole. These stripes are created by slowly pouring, with a small funnel, the powder glass towards the wall of the mold with alternating contrasting colors. The thickness of the stripes will depend on the amount of contrasting color used. For consistent layers, attention needs to be paid to the amount of powder glass poured between the stripes.

Horizontal-striped powder glass bead

Terrazzo Beads (*Te Mue*)

Terrazzo, also called stone beads, are made by crushing two or more different powder glass beads, mixing and re-firing them as part of a new bead. The first two layers (green and white) are powder glass, then the crushed beads are added in the mold, topping them again with another layer of powder glass. An alternative is to only use the crushed beads without adding any powder glass to it.

Terrazzo bead with powder glass

Vertical-Striped Beads (*Zagba or Adjiagba*)

These beads follow the same technique as the basic powder glass beads, except the design of these beads runs parallel to the bead hole. The mold is filled with a single powder glass color. Once the mold is filled, a very thin stick skewer or metal pin is inserted at the edge of the mold towards the wall of the mold and to the bottom. Using a small funnel, the small groove is slowly filled with a different contrasting powder glass color to create the design.

Vertical-striped powder glass bead

Vertical-Twisted Striped Beads (*Zagba Ne-Aki*)

These beads are created following the same process as the vertical-striped beads. Upon removing the mold from the kiln and while still hot, a metal pin is inserted into the bead hole. Pressing down and turning the pin in a clock-wise motion, using the second pin to stabilize the mold against the working surface to avoid tipping it over. The bead is then flipped over, pressed down and turned in a counter clock-wise motion. This will give the "S" shape twisted pattern. If the direction is not reversed while shaping the second half, a "C" shape pattern will be formed. These two motions need to happen while the bead is still hot. If the mold cools down to the point that the bead inside the mold cannot be rotated, it needs to be placed back in the kiln for another 15 minutes or more to be re-processed.

Vertical-twisted-striped powder glass bead

Vertical-Stripe Beads

1. Elements needed to make a vertical-stripe bead.

2. Powder glass poured above the cassava leaf stalk.

3. Vertical stripes are punched with a fine metal pin.

4. Holes are made for every intended stripe.

5. Holes are slowly filled with desired colors.

6. Compress by slightly tapping the mold.

7. Beads are shaped while glass is still hot.

8. Vertical-striped bead with 8 stripes.

Horizontal-Stripe Beads

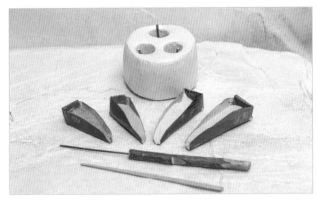

1. Elements needed to make a horizontal-stripe bead.

2. Powder glass poured above the cassava leaf stalk.

3. Holes are partially filled with bead base color.

4. Horizontal stripes are filled towards the edge.

5. Additional stripes are filled with desired color.

6. After last stripe, bead holes are filled with base color.

7. Beads are shaped while glass is still hot.

8. Horizontal-stripe bead with 5 layers.

Powder Glass Beads Gallery

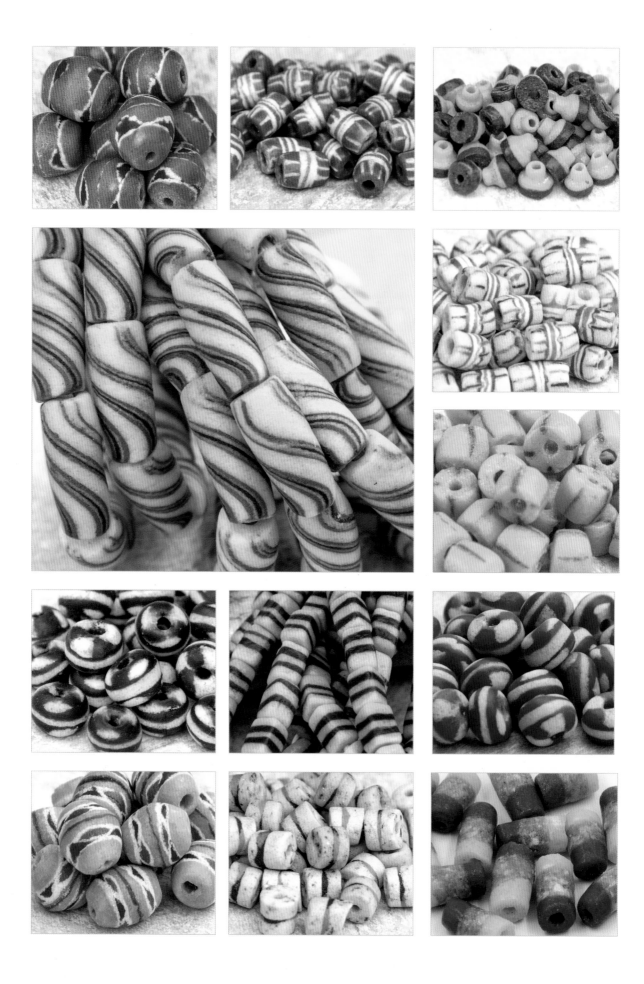

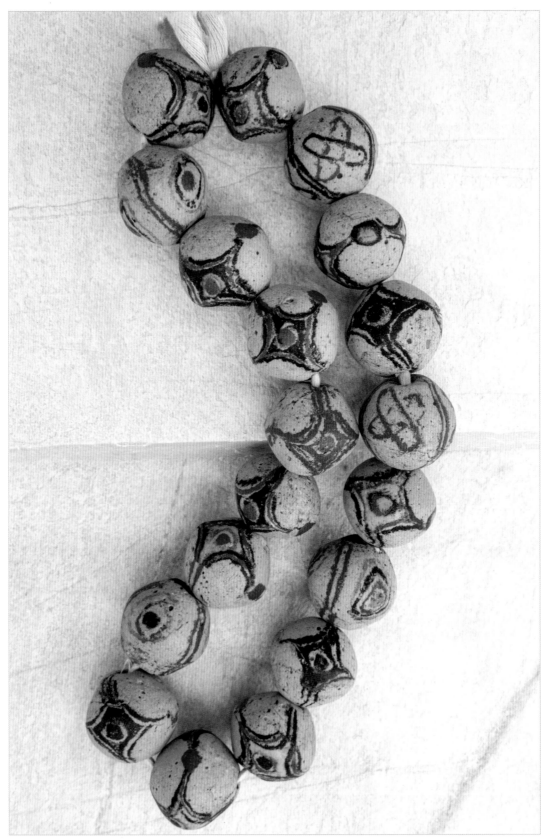

Akorso Bodom beads are special beads made for chiefs and queen mothers. Some of the preferred designs are the *Cruciform*, associated with the ancestors; *Alutoto (Turtle)*, a sacred creature that symbolizes long life and prosperity for Krobo bead makers; and *Zagba* or *Ajiagba* with vertical and diagonal stripes.

CHAPTER 8
Bodom Beads

Bodom beads are the ancestors of present-day powder glass beads in Ghana.

They are a type of powder glass beads once produced exclusively for chiefs and queen mothers used in diverse rites, ceremonies, and festivals.

They are the largest of the powder glass beads made in Ghana ranging from 20 to 50 mm (0.78 to 1.96 inches) in diameter.

The word *Bodom* means dog in the Akan language, as the *Bodom* bead seem to "*bark*" to be noticed. They are usually made with yellow-ochre or lemon-yellow powder glass, featuring a diamond shape on the outer skin, created by layering powder glass of different colors in the bead mold.

Bodom beads of a certain age and design are valuable and often considered to have magical or medicinal powers. They are used with pride in ceremonies, including funerals, and in traditional festivals and gatherings. They are passed down through generations as a valuable heirloom.

Although yellow is the preferred color by chiefs and queen mothers, nowadays *Bodom* beads are made in a variety of colors. *Akorso Bodom* beads are special beads made for chiefs and queen mothers.

How to make *Bodom* beads:

- Pour powder glass into the mold using the funnels.
- With help of a design pin, make 2 or 3 triangular piles of powder glass equally distant apart.
- Add on top of the triangular piles a layer of a different powder glass color to create the design.
- Add additional powder glass of the base color.
- Depending on the desired design of the *Bodom* bead, add other colors as needed.
- Once the mold is filled halfway, repeat the chosen design in a mirror image.
- After the mold is completely filled, use the handle of the design pin to gently tap the mold to settle the powder down.
- Usually, additional powder glass is added on top of the mold to compensate for the shrinkage during the firing.
- Place the mold in the kiln.
- Fire the bead for 20 to 35 minutes at 600° to 800° C (1112° to 1472° F).
- Shape the beads using the technique shown in *Chapter 14*.
- Follow the same cleaning and polishing steps as shown in *Chapter 15*.

Dexterity, skill, and patience is essential in the making of the *Bodom* bead.

Different funnel sizes are used depending on the amount of powder glass used for the main color and other design colors.

Bodom Bead Making Demonstration

Using a clear glass container, *Cedi* demonstrates the technique to make *Bodom* beads. In this example, he places a cassava leaf stalk as a place holder for the bead hole. Then he uses white powder glass for the base color and brown, green, and red for the center design. The powder is poured using a funnel.

Using the funnel and design pin, he makes 3 triangular piles of powder equally distant apart. Using the design pin, he pours the brown powder to outline the triangular shape. Then he adds more white powder glass. Depending on the desired design of the *Bodom* bead, other colors are added. After the mold is filled halfway, the chosen design is repeated in a mirror image.

After the mold is completely filled, he uses the handle of the design pin to gently tap the powder down. Usually, some more powder is added on top of the mold to compensate for the shrinkage during the firing at the kiln.

Bodom Beads Gallery

Translucent and Opaque Beads

Translucent and opaque beads are made from crushed glass, also called *frit*. These beads reflect the exact color of the glass used.

Translucent and Opaque Glazed Beads

Translucent or opaque beads are individually hand painted to produce a beautiful variety of beads.

CHAPTER 9

Translucent and Opaque Glass Beads

Translucent beads, known locally as *Korli*, are made from crushed glass, which is also called *frit*. After the bottle or scrap glass has been washed and dried, it is broken into smaller pieces to fit into the desired mold.

These beads reflect the exact color of the glass used. Some colors, like cobalt or red, are difficult to obtain as there are not many such colored bottles in Ghana. Green and brown from beer bottles is readily available.

Translucent or transparent beads made with fragments of broken glass or *frit* retain the translucency of glass, rather than the beads produced from finely powdered glass

Shaping is an important skill needed for making translucent beads. In a standard round bead, the center hole is pierced first. Pressing against the bottom of the mold, the bead maker shapes one side. The bead is then turned over, in the still hot mold, shaping the other side against the sides of the mold to give it the round shape.

How to make translucent glass beads:

- Place fragments in the mold.
- Place mold in the kiln for 30 to 45 minutes at a temperature of 800° to 1000° C (1472° to 1832° F).
- Remove the mold from the kiln.
- Use a pin to stabilize the mold against the working surface.
- Insert the other pin to make the bead hole while the glass is still hot or pliable.
- Lift the bead out of the mold using the other pin, pressing the hot glass against the mold sides in a circular motion to form the shape.
- Turn over the bead to shape the other side.
- Cool the bead inside the mold for about 1 hour or more, if needed, depending on the weather conditions.
- Shape the beads using the technique shown in *Chapter 14*.
- Follow the same cleaning and polishing steps as shown in *Chapter 15*.

Glass is broken with a small hammer.

Pieces of broken glass are placed in the mold.

Bead is molded using pins while glass is still hot.

Mold with glass pieces ready to be placed in the kiln.

Translucent and Opaque Glass Beads Gallery

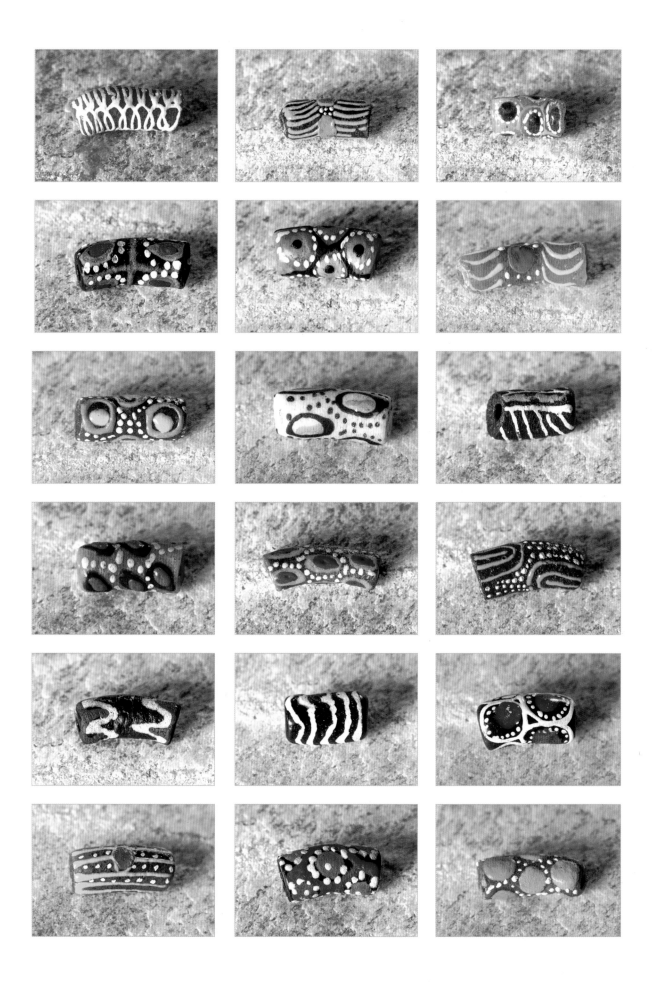

CHAPTER 10
Glazed, Painted, or Written Beads

Glazed beads, are also called painted or written beads because they are painted or written on. They are created by painting designs on either plain powder glass, translucent, or opaque glass beads. A mixture of powder glass, powdered ceramic dye/pigment, and water is used.

After the initial firing, these beads are stacked on a thin wooden stick to be painted or glazed.

After the painted surface has dried, each bead is placed back in the mold and fired for the required additional time.

These beads are very popular as this method can provide a much richer variety of designs than the powder glass beads.

These beads also allow for a faster production than the intricate powder glass design beads.

How to make glazed glass beads:

- Once the beads have cooled down, stack them in a thin wooden stick.
- Apply the color mixture by hand to each bead using a thin stick or syringe like pen.
- Designs vary from very simple lines to very elaborate multicolor designs.
- Let the color mixture dry naturally.
- Once dried, place them back into the mold and fire them again for approx. 20 to 30 minutes at 482° to 538° C (900° to 1000° F) to allow the mixture to fuse to the bead.
- Let the beads cool down for about 1 hour.
- Wash beads with water and soap or with very fine sand for just a few minutes before applying lubricant oil or Vaseline.

Glazed, painted, or written beads allow for a faster production than powder glass designs.

A mixture of powder glass, ceramic dye, and water is used to paint the beads.

Hand-painted beads are made using a thin stick, syringe, or needle to apply the mixture.

Glazed, Painted, or Written Beads Gallery

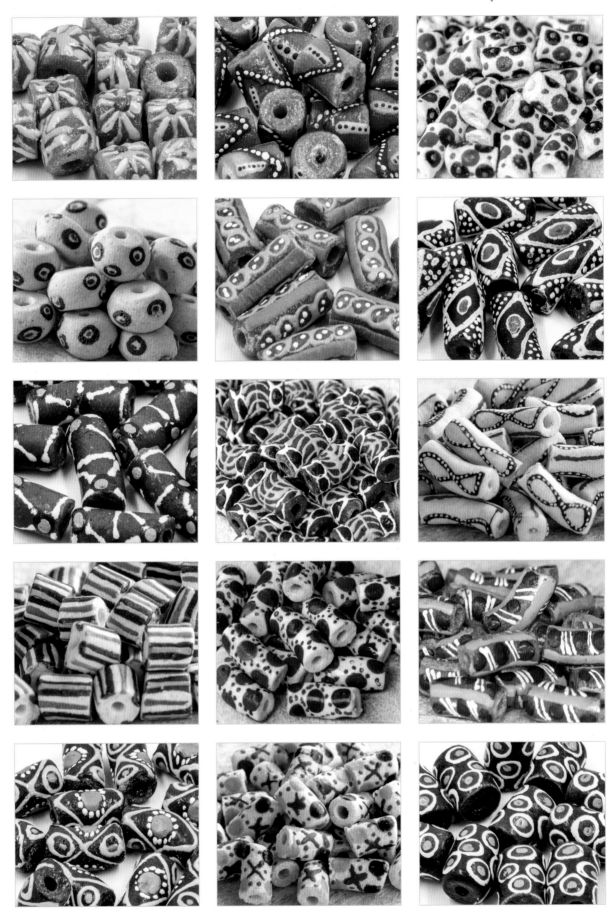

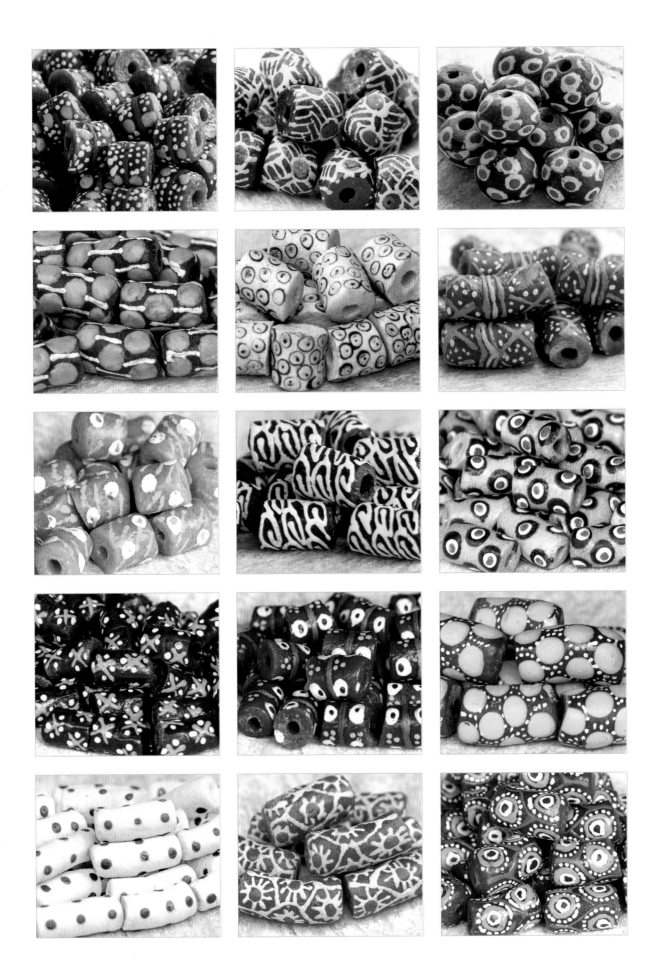

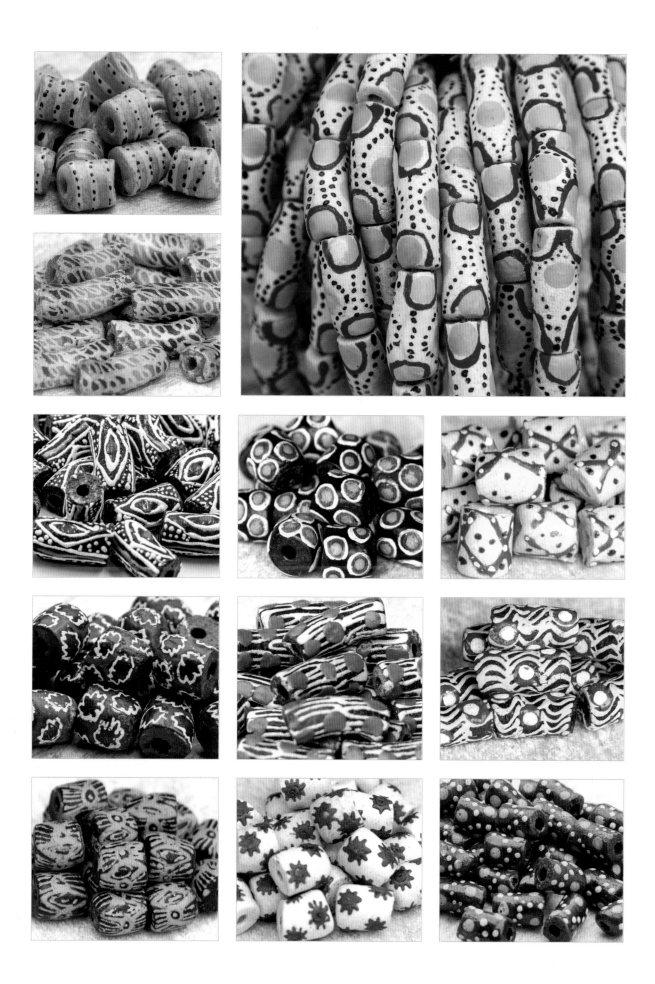

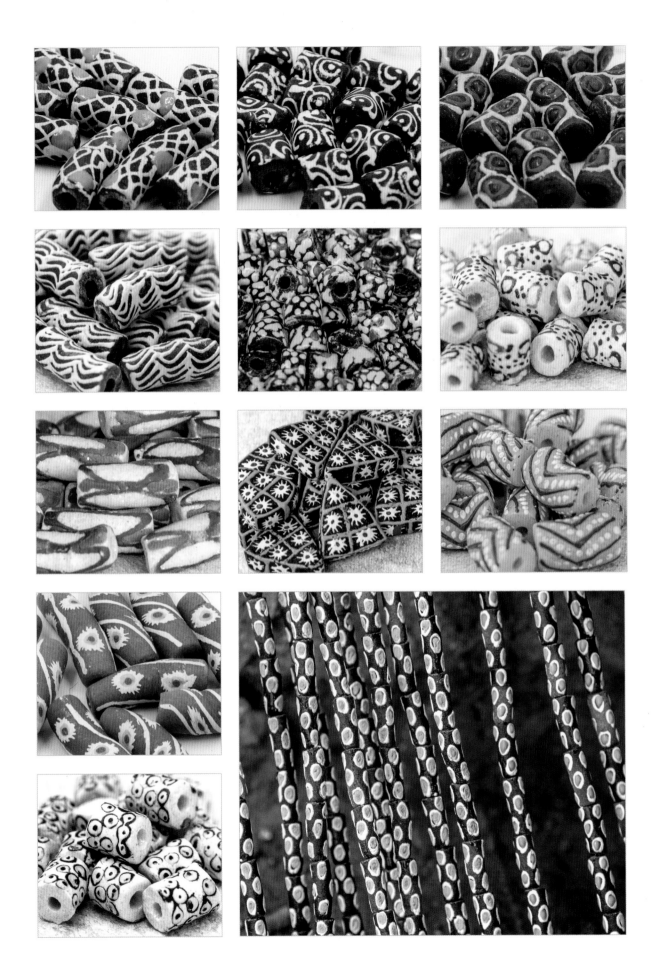

Cassava leaf stalk is carefully placed in each hole.

A small funnel is used to pour the powder glass.

Seed or waist bead making requires skill and patience due to their small size.

The meaning of the colors of seed or waist beads

Black	Power /Protection
Blue	Loyalty/Truth
Brown	Earth/Stability
Gold	Good Health/Power/Wealth
Green	Abundance/Fertility/Nature/Prosperity
Orange	Courage/Self-Confidence/Vitality
Pink	Care/ Beauty/Love/Kindness
Purple	Royalty/Spirituality/Wisdom
Red	Confidence/Vitality
Turquoise	Communication/Self-Awareness
White	Light/Truth/Purity
Yellow	Energy/Joy/Happiness

CHAPTER 11
Seed or Waist Beads

Seed or waist beads are made using the same technique as the regular powder glass beads with the size being the only difference. The mold has small holes, and a tiny cassava leaf stalk is placed in each one. Once the cassava leaf stalk are in place, powder glass is poured to fill all holes.

Seed or waist beads are also known as *belly beads* and are used for symbolic adornment by women. The beads are embedded in a long string and tied just below the navel. They serve as a sign of wealth, and to draw attention to, and enhance, their femininity.

During naming ceremonies babies are typically adorned with waist beads. Since traditional waist beads are strung on a cotton cord without a clasp they are also a good tool to measure weight gain and loss.

How to make seed or waist beads:

- Place a small cassava leaf stalk in each hole of the mold.
- Fill mold with powder glass in the desired color.
- Place mold in the kiln for about 45 minutes.
- Remove the mold from the kiln while the cassava leaf stalk burns away and the glass is still hot, placing it on the floor to let it cool down naturally.
- Cool the beads inside the mold for about 1 hour.
- These beads are also polished as shown in *Chapter 14*.

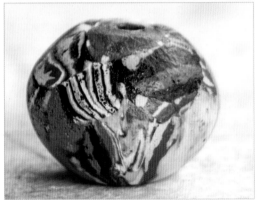

Broken pieces are washed and sorted into matching types and color combinations. These beads are also called *End-of-the-day* beads.

Recycled old damaged or broken glass beads have been part of the Krobo bead repertoire for decades but have become increasingly popular in recent years specially in the export market.

CHAPTER 12
Recycled Broken Beads

Over centuries, broken glass beads from Europe were discarded as scrap. In the 1950s, the Krobo realized that these antique or old broken or damaged beads could be recycled into new beads.

Currently, there are bead traders that sell old broken beads to bead makers to be recycled into new beads. New broken beads can also be used.

The broken pieces are washed and sorted into matching types and color combinations to obtain the best results in producing a new bead.

Separation by color and design will allow complementary combinations for the new recycled bead. Many times, the result is a beautiful mosaic bead showing the design and color of the original beads used.

Beads that are cracked or only partially broken or damaged are also used in the melting process to create interesting and look-alike old beads.

Consideration needs to be given to the glass type of the old bead to avoid conflicts in the glass re-transitioning or fusing process.

How to make broken recycled glass beads:

- Choose the broken pieces you want to combine, making sure the pieces you choose are compatible glass types for the re-transitioning or fusing process.
- Place them in the desired mold.
- Place the mold in the kiln.
- The temperature to fire these beads is similar to the temperature used for *frit*.
- Shape the beads using the technique shown in *Chapter 14*.
- Follow the same cleaning and polishing steps as shown in *Chapter 15*.

Old or new broken glass beads are recycled to make new beads following a similar technique as *frit*. Attention needs to be given to make sure the types of glass to be re-transitioned or fused are compatible with one another.

Recycled Broken Beads Gallery

Seed beads of different sizes and colors are combined to produce recycled new beads.

New imported seed beads are recycled into new colorful beads of various sizes and shapes. Some seed beads are made by mixing crushed glass or powder glass with seed beads.

CHAPTER 13
Recycled Seed Beads

The use of broken or damaged glass beads to make new beads has, in recent years, extended to using new seed or waist imported glass seed beads from Asia and Europe to produce a new bead type.

Since the imported seed beads are made of soft glass, the glass transition temperature is lower than the powder glass, requiring less firing time.

The combinations made possible using seed beads are as vast as the bead maker's imagination and taste for color combinations. Some seed beads are made by mixing crushed glass or powder glass with seed beads.

These new type of beads have in recent years become very popular, especially among tourists and in the export market.

How to make recycled seed beads:

- Choose the seed beads you want to mix.
- Place them in the desired mold.
- To place the seed beads into the mold, use a small cup to provide a consistent amount.
- Place the mold in the kiln.
- Since the imported seed beads are made of soft glass, the glass transition temperature is lower than the powder glass.
- Shape the beads using the technique shown in *Chapter 14*.
- Follow the same cleaning and polishing steps as shown in *Chapter 15*.

Seed beads are placed in the mold using a small cup to obtain a consistent bead size.

Seed beads are placed in the mold by hand.

Molds with seed beads are carefully placed in the kiln for firing.

Recycled Seed Beads Gallery

When the bead is in a gum stage, attention needs to be given not to press the pin too much, otherwise it will leave a mark on the bead.

Great skill is needed when several beads are in a mold to shape them while the glass is still hot and before it cools down.

All beads in the mold need to be leveled so that the bead hole is straight and without sharp edges. Sharp bead edges may cut the thread during or after stringing them.

CHAPTER 14
Bead Shaping

Each bead is individually shaped. Depending on the final shape desired, a slightly different technique is applied.

Using the metal pins, beads are shaped or flattened into round, bi-cone, barrel shape, or flat beads.

This is a laborious manual task as each bead is shaped one by one by the bead artisan.

The shaping of the bead requires experience and dexterity acquired by the artisans after years of practice.

How to shape glass beads:

- Take the mold out of the kiln.
- Insert one of the metal pins where the skewer burned away.
- The second pin is used to stabilize the mold against the working surface.
- Lift the bead out of the mold using the other pin while pressing the hot bead with a circular motion against the sides of the mold to give it the desired shape.
- Turn over the bead, in the still hot mold, to shape the other side of it against the sides of the mold to give it the final shape.
- Observe caution during this process to prevent burns.

One of the pins is inserted where the cassava leaf stalk is burned away to re-dress the bead hole.

The bead is lifted using one of the pins while pressing the bead against the sides of the mold.

Grinding a powder glass bead with an electric grinder.

Polishing beads on a grinding stone.

Beads should not be ground too long on one side to prevent forming flat spots.

Beads are periodically rinsed in a bucket of water to monitor the progress.

CHAPTER 15
Bead Cleaning and Polishing

Once the beads are at room temperature, and can be handled by hand they are cleaned and polished. Beads may still have irregularities and/or residue of kaolin from the mold.

This is a labor intensive process and is done by most bead artisans by hand on a smooth stone using soft sand and water.

As technology enters the bead manufacturing process, more and more bead makers are also using electric polishing drums or grinders. For grinding, a medium grade diamond hand pad and water may also be used. A grinder is also used to give final shape to beads with trapezoid form. This process will ensure that the beads are clean, smooth, and display the full brightness of their colors.

How to clean and polish beads:

- Mix sand and water onto the grinding surface.
- Rub the beads in a back and forth motion to remove impurities.
- Make sure to lift the tip of your fingers in this process to prevent damaging your fingers.
- Rotate the beads and repeat until all beads are clean and smooth.
- Avoid rubbing the beads too long on one side to prevent flat spots.
- Rinse beads periodically to monitor progress.
- After the beads have been cleaned and dried, the glass may occasionally give a cloudy appearance.
- To eliminate the cloudy appearance you will see on some beads, rub the beads with a thin coat of multi-purpose oil, baby oil, or Vaseline to enhance the colors giving them a satin sheen look.
- Make sure to wipe off any excess oil.

Some beads are polished using an electric grinder or tumbler.

Multi-purpose oil, baby oil, or Vaseline can be used to coat the beads to help display the full brightness of their colors.

Recycled seed beads are strung according to their size and type for distribution.

Glazed beads are strung for necklaces and bracelets for the export market.

Strung powder glass beads ready for bulk export.

CHAPTER 16
Bead Stringing and Quality Control

Once the beads have been polished, washed, dried, and oiled, they are sorted by color and shape for easier handling. The sorted beads are then strung with yarn or raffia, making them ready for sale. Ghana is currently exporting recycled glass beads to many countries around the world.

From the first step of the manufacturing process to the stringing in bundles for distribution and sale, manual labor is an integral part of the glass bead production.

Ghanaian recycled glass beads, antique and new, are currently popular around the globe as accessories as well as collectibles. They are worn as bracelets, necklaces, earrings, pendants, and adorn clothing. Their colors and shapes, either as a simple string of beads or as the most sophisticated necklaces, are captivating.

Stringing beads as necklaces or bracelets is done manually by skilled workers.

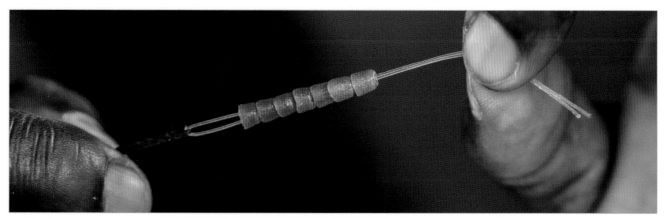

Due to their size, seed or waist beads, are strung using a thin nylon string.

 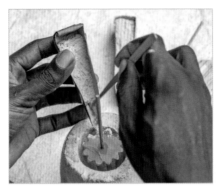 

1. Using a special mold for *Chevron* beads, the largest *dented cone* is placed in the center of the mold equidistant from the internal mold wall. Once the mold is filled and tapped, the cone is removed.

2. The second largest cone is then carefully inserted, maintaining the same distance all around the powder glass wall. White powder glass is poured around the cone. Once done, it is tapped and the cone removed.

3. Successively insert one after the other the smaller size cones, pouring each time the desired powder glass color, alternating with white powder glass each time. Maintain a steady hand during the whole process.

4. Once the smallest cone is used, extract the cone and place a cassava leaf stalk in the center of the hole and pour the last layer of powder glass. Tap the mold slightly against the working surface to compact the powder glass.

CHAPTER 17
Chevron, Rosetta, or Star Beads

Chevron, Rosetta, or Star beads are known as *Powa* beads in the *Ga-Adangme* language. They are among the most valuable and noble trade beads, often called the *"aristocrat of beads"* and considered by many the most popular bead in history with over a hundred variations.[1]

This type of bead was originally created by glass bead makers in Venice and Murano, Italy, toward the end of the 14th century. Chevron beads were brought to West Africa by Dutch merchants around the 15th century.

Chevrons are specialized cane or drawn-glass beads with a number of concentric layers of colored powder glass. Chevrons are usually blue with white and red stripes. The number of layers increases its complexity and therefore the value of the bead.

Venetian Technique:

- These canes are formed by forcing or blowing a single or multiple layered gather of glass into a tapered mold with a zigzag pattern, thus producing points on its outer surface.
- This pleated gather is then encased with additional glass layers of various colors.
- The short cylinders are then cut, and the ends are beveled or ground down to reveal the zigzags or stars of the bead.

Local Technique:

- It follows the same technique as the powder glass beads, requiring a large special mold and special tools.

Only beads with ground ends, either faceted, rounded, or chamfered, and with their inner layers exposed, are properly called *Chevron* beads. All *Star* beads with flat ends are called *Rosetta* beads.

Cedi learned the special technique of *Chevron* beads from *Art Seymour*, a famous master bead maker from Nevada in the United Sates, and also during his trips to Venice and Murano in Italy.

---

1 Janet Coles & Robert Budwing, *The Complete Book of Beads*, p. 23.

Chevron, Rosetta, or Star Beads Gallery

Materials, tools and equipment are totally different than those used for the traditional recycled glass bead making.

Samples of flame- or torch-worked beads created by *Cedi* in his workshop in Odumase.

CHAPTER 18
Lamp-, Flame-, or Torch-Worked Beads

Cedi is the first artisan in Ghana to use the flame- or torch-worked technique to make beads, requiring totally different equipment, tools, and materials than the ones used for powder glass bead making.

Lamp-, flame-, or torch-worked is a type of glass work where oxygen and propane are mixed to create a flame through a blow torch to help the glass transition. Once in a viscous or rubbery state, the glass is shaped with special tools and hand movements.

Cedi's initiative to make lamp-, flame-, or torch-worked beads was an important step for the bead industry in Ghana.

Distinctive traditional patterns and color combinations make *Cedi's* torch-worked creations truly works of art.

With his great talent and vast experience as a master bead maker, *Cedi* combines various techniques to create his flame-worked beads.

Lamp-, Flame-, or Torch-worked Beads Gallery

With steady hands, patience, creativity, and passion under the flame of the torch, in his studio *Cedi* produces beads worthy of royalty. These beads combine a traditional design known as *Akorso Bodom* with lamp-worked beads.

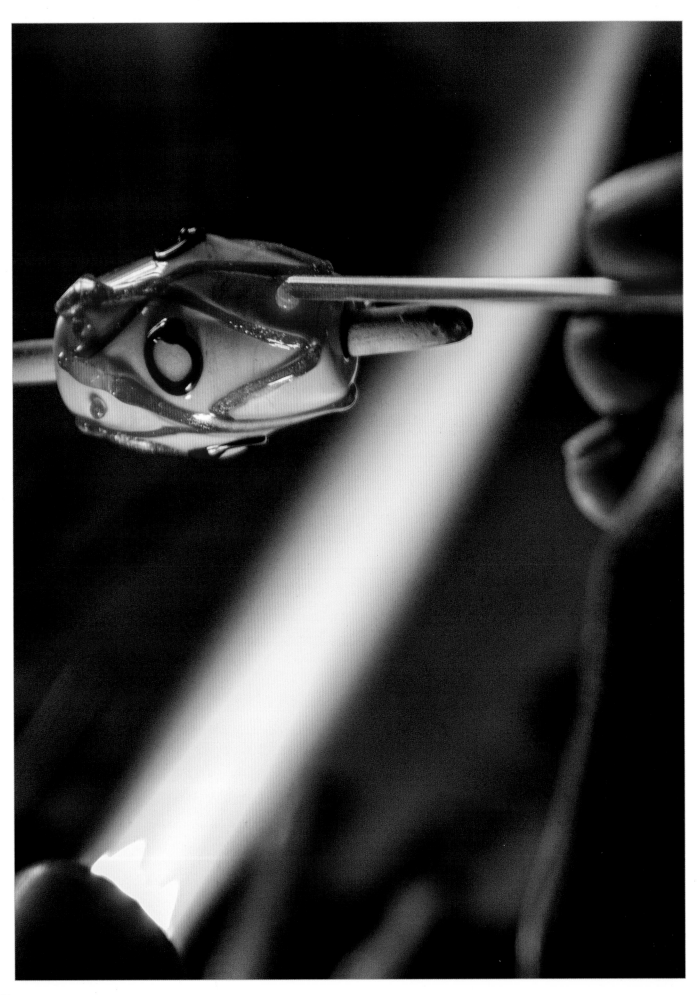

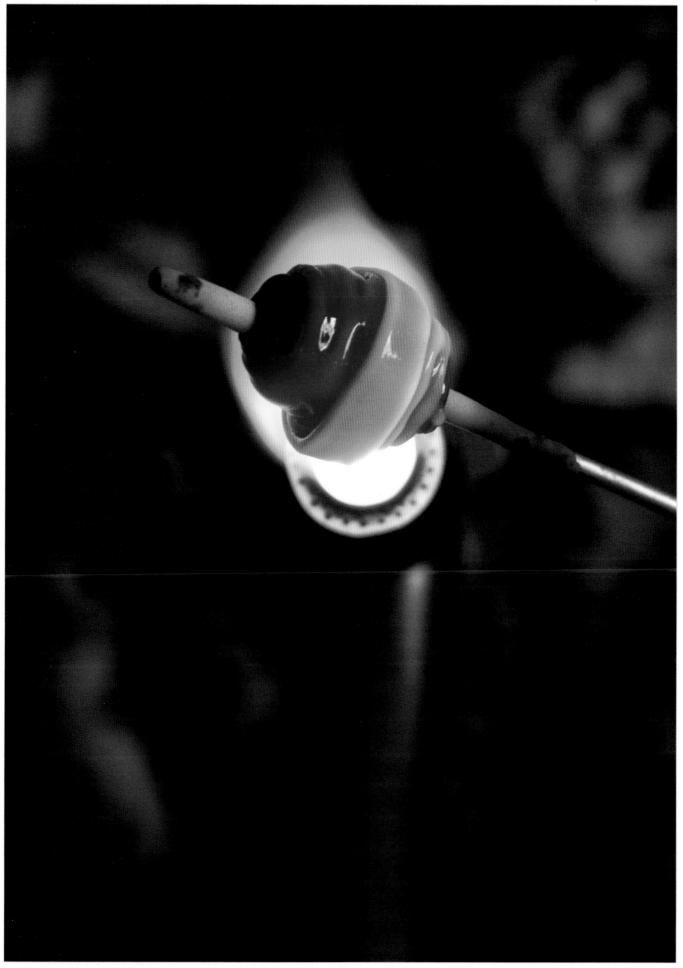

Triangular shape earrings are made with a hole in the apex of the triangle where a ring can be inserted.

Specialty buttons are used in fashion clothing designs and as home decorations.

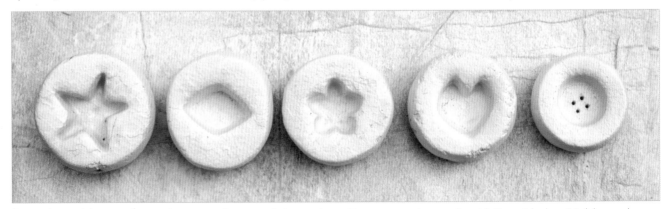

Specialty molds to make earrings, pendants, and decorations. Buttons can be made with 2 or 4 holes. Molds can be designed for any kind of glass accessories.

CHAPTER 19
Recycled Glass Accessories

In addition to beads, powder glass offers a range of possibilities using the same elements and techniques as powder glass beads. Over the years, new objects come and go as per the demand of local and international users.

Among the objects produced over the years by *Cedi*, we find powder glass buttons, earrings, pendants, and decoration artifacts used by clothing designers and decorators.

These objects basically follow the same technique as explained in *Chapter 3 - Recycled Glass*. The main difference is in the molds used to produce the desired shapes.

These special accessories can be made in the form of flowers, fish, hearts, stars, and many other shapes as per the design of the mold.

These specialized powder glass accessories do not need to be shaped after the firing.

Buttons are in demand by clothing companies specializing in African wear.

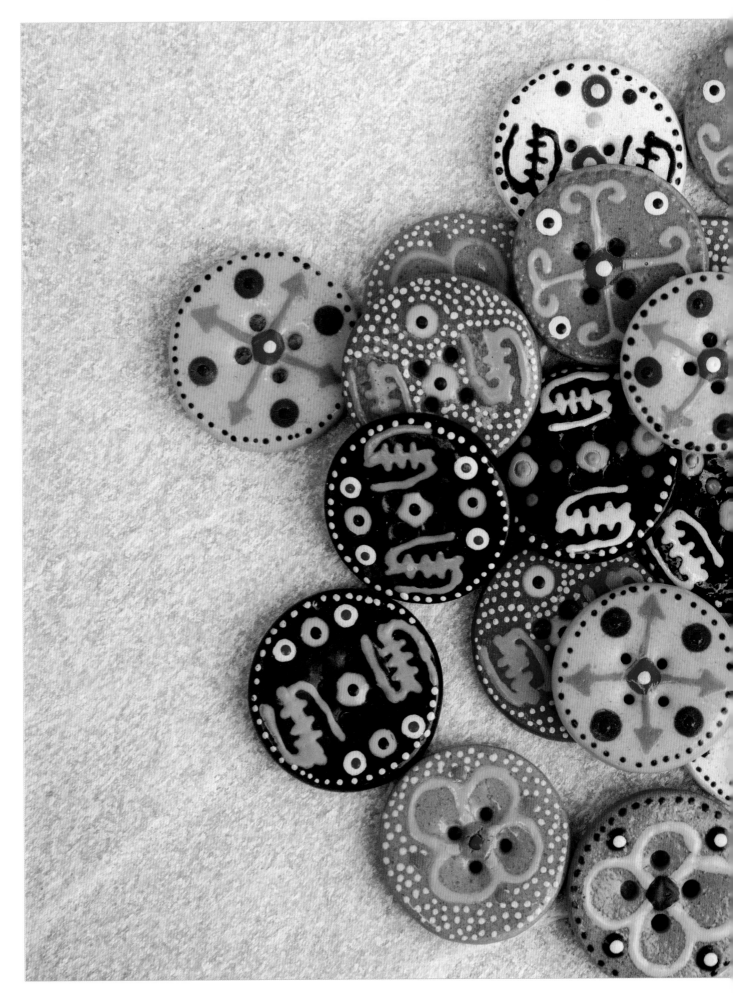

Glass Bottles

Scrap Glass

Crushed Glass/*Frit*

Powder Glass

Specialty Bead

Powder Chevron

Frit Translucent

Frit Opaque

Frit Opaque

Powder Bodom

Powder Vertical Twisted Stripe

Powder Horizontal-Stripe

Frit Translucent Glazed

Frit Opaque Glazed

Frit Translucent Button

Powder Bi-cone

Powder Glazed Eye Bead

Powder Glazed Cylinder

Powder/*Frit* Flat ring

Powder/*Frit* Rounded Bi-cone

Powder/*Frit* Terrazzo

Powder/*Frit* Terrazzo

Although the combinations of different types of glass are basically endless, this chart intends to provide an overview and reference of the composition of some of the most common recycled glass beads. A relatively recent trend among bead makers in Ghana is the fusing of seed beads with crushed or powder glass into new types of beads.

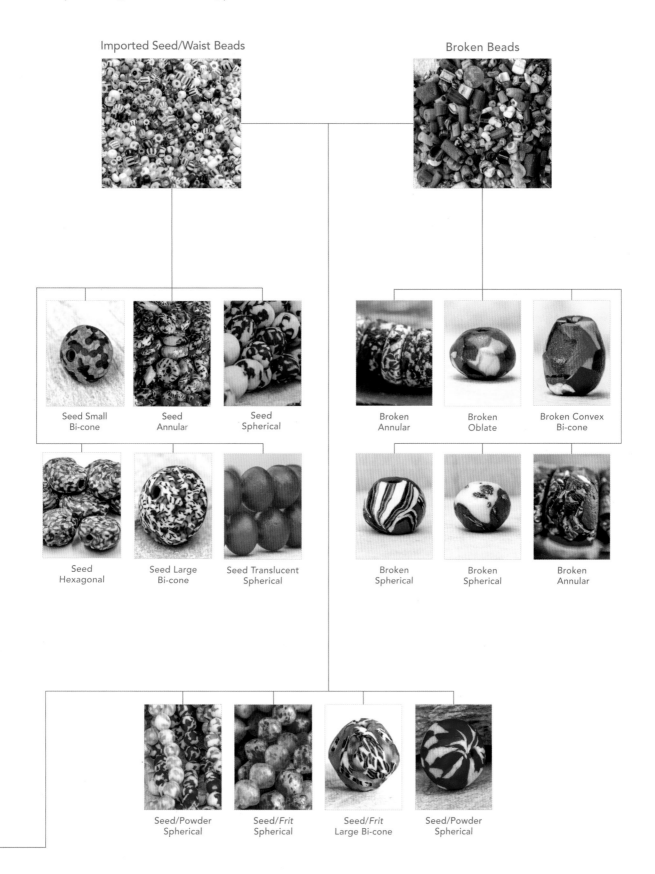

Imported Seed/Waist Beads

Broken Beads

Seed Small
Bi-cone

Seed
Annular

Seed
Spherical

Broken
Annular

Broken
Oblate

Broken Convex
Bi-cone

Seed
Hexagonal

Seed Large
Bi-cone

Seed Translucent
Spherical

Broken
Spherical

Broken
Spherical

Broken
Annular

Seed/Powder
Spherical

Seed/Frit
Spherical

Seed/Frit
Large Bi-cone

Seed/Powder
Spherical

CHAPTER 21

Glass Beads Shapes and Sizes

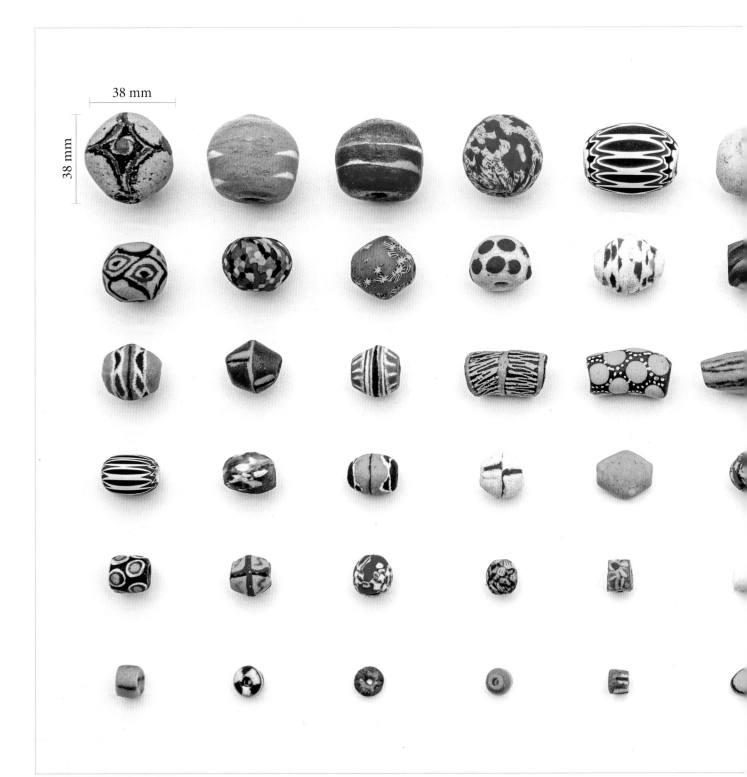

The shape and size of the bead plays a role as important as the color. Far from being uniformly small round objects, beads are made in a large range of different sizes and shapes. The shapes and sizes shown in this chart are the most representative of the beads made in Ghana. Beads are always measured through the diameter in millimeters. The examples in the following *Glass Beads Shapes and Sizes Chart* are an *Akorso Bodom* bead measuring 38 mm by 38 mm and a *Seed* bead measuring 3 mm by 2.8 mm.

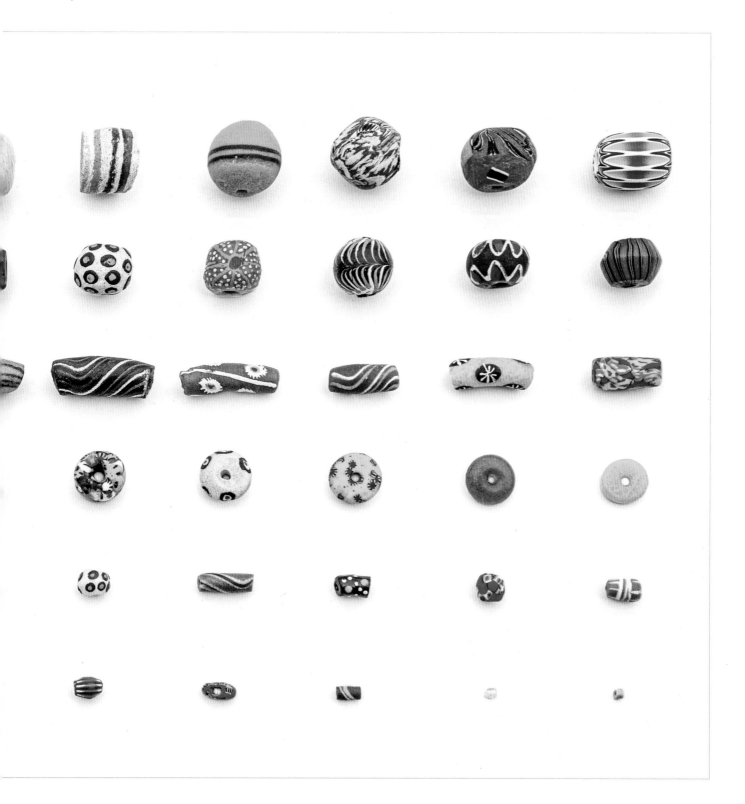

CHAPTER 22
A Master Bead Maker

In Odumase Krobo, the capital of the Manya Krobo kingdom, a quaint township nestled at the foot of the Akuapem-Togo mountains in the Eastern Region of Ghana, lives an internationally-recognized and well-respected master bead maker, *Nomoda Ebenezer Djaba,* better known as *Cedi.* His wife, *Mariama Djaba,* has fully supported him throughout his succesful career.

Cedi is a descendant of a long line of Krobo bead makers. Working alongside his family, he began designing powder glass beads at the age of seven.

The vast knowledge about the art of recycled glass bead making he has acquired over the past 40 years allows him to know and work in every facet of the process, including the art of Torch-worked beads and the labor intensive *Chevron* beads.

His innovative designs and techniques, as well as his passion for the craft, have taken him to many countries around the world to exhibits,

conferences, art fairs, shows, and workshops where he has conducted educational and professional demonstrations of the art of recycled glass bead making. In Ghana he has been to the University of Ghana, Legon; Kwame Nkrumah University of Science and Technology, Kumasi; University of Education, Winneba; University of Cape Coast, Cape Coast; Ho Polytechnic, Ho; St. Theresa Training College, Hohoe; St. Francis Training College, Hohoe; Jasikan College of Education, Jasikan.

Internationally, he has led workshops, among many others, at Cornell University, Ithaca, New York, USA; Iowa University, Iowa City, USA; Bullseye Glass, Portland Oregon, USA; Penland School of Craft, Mitchell County, North Carolina, USA; Finland Craft School, Helsinki, Finland; University of Kassel, Witzenhausen, Germany; International Festival of Glass, Stourbridge, England; and also in Botswana, Burkina Faso, Ethiopia, Namibia, Netherlands, Tanzania, Switzerland, United Kingdom, Zambia, and Zimbabwe.

Cedi made presentations at the International Folk Art in Santa Fe, New Mexico, USA; the International Folk Art Market Collection Show, Dallas, USA; the Rocky Mountains Gem Show, Denver, USA; Bead Bazaar, Witzenhausen Museum, Germany; Expo 2010, Shanghai, China; International Society of Glass Beadmakers Conference, Rochester NY, USA; Trunk Show: Bead Art Resources, Newton, MA, USA; Trunk Show: 10,000 Villages, Ithaca, NY, USA; Higuchi Palace Theater, Glass Fashion Show, Corning, NY, USA; California Gift Show, Los Angeles, USA. Palexpo Hall-Golden Ghana, Geneva, Switzerland; Bead Bazaar International Society of Glass Beadmakers, Boston, MA, USA; Glass Art Society, Seattle, WA, USA; Glass Art Society (GAS), Corning, New York, USA; Bead Bazaar, Bern and Liestal, Switzerland;

Throughout his lengthy career, he has been awarded Certificates of Appreciation, Honor, Excellence, and Achievement from prestigious institutions. In 2018 he won the *Living Tradition Award* in Santa Fe, NM, USA.

Over the years, he has welcomed to his factory in Odumase Krobo thousands of visitors. In 2017, *Margrethe II, Queen of Denmark* visited the factory where *Cedi* personally showed her several aspects of the bead production.

Cedi has appeared in several television programs in Africa and Europe and his work as well as accomplishments has been featured in many books, magazines, and newspaper articles around the globe, recognizing him as a prominent bead maker: *The Art & Tradition of Beadwork* by Marsha C. Bol; *Glass Fashion Extravaganza* by Laura Donefer; *Santa Fe International Folk Art Market 2014 Book*; *Schätze Aus Feuer und Sand* by Treppen Keller Hinterhöfe; *African Beads: Jewels of a Continent* by Evelyn Simak and Carl Dreibelbis, edited by Lois Sherr Dubin; *Gender and Change in the Krobo Bead Industry* by Amanda Kay Gilvin; *Ghana: Where the Bead Speaks* by Esi Sutherland-Addy and Kati Torda Dagadu. *The Bead is Constant,* edited by Alexandra Wilson, 2003. *Ornament Magazine*, Vol. 26.3, 2003.

Cedi is the President of the Manya Krobo Bead Association and a founding member of the Ghana Bead Society. He is also the Vice Chairman of the Ghana Association of Visual Artists, Eastern Region. He has also served as a member of the International Society of Glass Beadmakers, USA.

Nomoda Ebenezer Djaba and a group of Krobo girls dressed in their traditional outfits adorned with the famous recycled glass beads produced by *Cedi Beads Industry.*

Glossary

Annealing—The process of slowly cooling hot glass objects after they have been formed, to relieve residual internal stress introduced during manufacturing.

Anlo—The Anlo Ewe are a sub-group of the Ewe people in the southeastern part of the Volta Region of Ghana.

Ashanti—People of an ethnic group in the Ashanti Region of Ghana.

Bisque Firing—A 3 day firing that forces all the water to leave the object and transform the clay into (almost) stone.

Bodom bead—A type of powder glass beads used mainly by chiefs and queen mothers.

Cassava leaf stalk—The cassava plant is a woody plant with erect stems and spirally arranged simple lobed leaves with leaf stalk up to 30 cm in length.

Cathedral glass—The name given commercially to monochromatic sheets of glass.

Chevron bead—A type of glass bead with 3 to 7 layers, originally invented in about 1500 by the Venetians. In the 17th century, the Dutch also manufactured Chevrons.

COE—Coefficient of Thermal Expansion.

Dipo—A Ghanaian traditional puberty rite among the *Ga-Adangme* people, mainly the people of Odumase Krobo and Yilo Krobo in the Eastern Region of Ghana. The puberty rite is used to usher girls into womanhood.

Ga-Adangme—An ethnic group in Ghana. The Ga and Dangbe people are grouped as part of an ethno-linguistic group and are an ethnic group that lives primarily in the Greater Accra and part of the Eastern Region of Ghana.

Glass transition temperature—The temperature range where the glass changes from a rigid to a soft (not melted) material, and is usually measured in terms of the stiffness. Also referred as the "melting point."

Krobo—People of an ethnic group in the Eastern Region of Ghana originally from the Krobo mountains.

Millefiori—A glass-work technique which produces distinctive decorative patterns on glassware. The term *millefiori* is a combination of the Italian words "mille" (thousand) and "fiori" (flowers).

Odumase—Capital of the Manya Krobo kingdom or Traditional Area in the Eastern Region of Ghana.

Pyrometer—A type of remote-sensing thermometer used to measure temperature.

Seed bead—Uniformly round-shaped tiny glass beads ranging in size from under a millimeter to several millimeters.

Traditional kings and queen mothers—In Ghana almost every town and village has a chief, sometimes called a king, and queen mothers who rule alongside the modern political system.

Waist bead—Traditional African accessory that consists of small glass beads on a string or wire worn around the waist or hips.

Wound bead—Molten glass wound around a steel wire called mandrel, following one of the earliest techniques in glass bead making.

References

Bugarin, Carol & Djaba, Nomoda, *Making Krobo Style Powder Glass Beads.* July 2010.

Tekuor Ackam, Nancy Leoca, *Amplifying the Ghanaian Bead Through Publication Design.* Thesis, School of Graduate Studies, Kwame Nkrumah University of Science and Technology, Kumasi. May, 2013.

Gott, Suzanne, *Ghana's Glass Beadmaking Arts in Transcultural Dialogues.* African Arts, Spring 2014, Vol. 47 No. 1.

Dubin, Lois Sherr, *The History of Beads*, Abradale Press, 1998.

Tomalin, Stefany, *Beads, A History and Collectors Guide*, Amberly, 2016.

Coles, Janet & Budwig, Robert, *The Complete Book of Beads*, Dorling Kindersley, London, *1990.*

Kradolfer, Philippe & Regula, *Ghanaian Recycled Glass Beads, From Used Glass to New Beads*, Ghana-Art Publications, 2018.

ACKNOWLEDGMENTS

We express sincere gratitude to the following for their generous support in making this publication possible:

LYNETTE N. GAY
ENSIGN COLLEGE OF PUBLIC HEALTH
ENGAGE NOW AFRICA

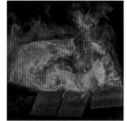

About the Authors

Nomoda E. Djaba and Philippe J. Kradolfer at *Cedi's*
workshop in Odumase Krobo.

Philippe learned to appreciate the Krobo recycled glass beads while attending many local ceremonies and traditional festivals. In 2019 he became an apprentice of Cedi.
As a photographer and designer, he has worked closely with *Cedi* documenting the process of the Krobo recycled glass beads. Philippe and his wife, Regula, Swiss and US citizens, live currently in Utah, USA. Prior to moving to the USA they lived in Switzerland, Bolivia, Peru, Ecuador, Mexico, Germany, Russia, Argentina, and Ghana. They were appointed in 2015 *Ewe Kente Ambassadors* for the Agotime Traditional Area in the Volta Region of Ghana, where they are known as *Nene Dunenyo I* and as *Manye Zevideka I*. Their passion for Ghana and its traditions has contributed to the publishing of several photo-documentaries such as: *Ghana Everyday Life*; *Unveiling the Volta Region of Ghana* (co-authored with Togbe Afede XIV); *Amufest* (co-authored with Osie Adza Tekpor VII), *Agotime Kente Festival* (co-authored with his daughter Michèle K. Morford); *2015 Asogli State Yam Festival*; *The Kente Store; and Ghanaian Recycled Glass Beads* (Co-authored with his wife).

The Art of Recycled Glass Beads

Ghana-Art Publications Ltd & EPP Books Services
©2020   ISBN 978-1-7923-2241-9